Christmas
the season to be jolly

This book is dedicated to Father Christmas and all the women who make his myth reality every year.

First published in the United Kingdom in 2017 by
Portico
43 Great Ormond Street
London
WC1N 3HZ

An imprint of Pavilion Books Company Ltd

ISBN 978-1-91104-254-9

A CIP catalogue record for this book is available from the British Library.

10 9 8 7 6 5 4 3 2

Reproduction by Mission Productions Ltd, Hong Kong
Printed and bound by Toppan Leefung Printing Ltd, China

This book can be ordered direct from the publisher at www.pavilionbooks.com

THE WIT AND
Cath Tate
WISDOM OF

Christmas

the season to be jolly

PORTICO

"Three Wise Men? Are you serious?"

Three Wise
Women
would have asked
directions, arrived
on time, delivered
the baby, cleaned
the stable, made a
casserole…

and there would
have been
Peace on Earth.

Christmas.
Mother can't contain her
excitement.

'Tis the season to be jolly.

"Yes mother, I will remember that Christmas is on the 25th December this year."

"Yes dear, I know it's Easter, but what do you want for Christmas?"

"You want WHAT for Christmas?"

"3 ½ hours to Christmas. Now, where shall I start?"

A MAN'S GUIDE TO PRESENTS
1) December 24th. Panic.

2) Find shop open. Buy everything.

3) 9.30pm. Three presents short. Panic.

4) Christmas morning. Rush to petrol station: chocolates, novelty lighter, brake fluid. Panic.

5) Find paper. Wrap.

6) Ta-dah! Nothing to it.

Fall asleep in front of the Queen's Speech.

A GRANNY'S GUIDE TO PRESENTS

1) December 26th. Go to the sales. Buy everything.

2) Iron last year's paper, wrap and hide.

3) August 1st. Ring everyone and ask them what they want for Christmas.

4) December 24th. Panic. Hunt for the presents, swap and relabel.

5) Christmas Day. Ta-dah! Nothing to it. Watch Queen.

Christmas is the time to let your hair down...

...and really sparkle.

“You drive.
I've got to drink.”

The trouble with the office party is finding a new job in the morning.

A Christmas party without alcohol is just a meeting.

"Full of Christmas spirit: gin, vodka, rum and brandy."

Christmas is so close you
can almost smell
the relatives.

"Yes, we ARE coming to stay with you this year."

Now's the time to lace your cooking with all those disgusting drinks you bought on holiday.

Finally you can relax while the men get all the important jobs done.

Christmas is the time to catch up with the odd relative.

A family is for life,
not just for Christmas.

"I'm sorry your presents are late this year. I had to travel Southern Reindeers."

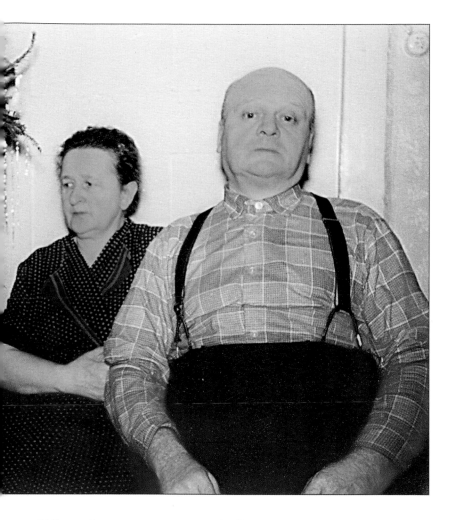

Christmas without
presents is just boring.

"I've been really good this year but my little brother's been really naughty."

'Tis the season to be greedy.

"Unfortunately
the dog found the presents
before we did."

"What on *earth* has he got me this time?"

Sometimes you don't get given what you want, you get given what you deserve.

Never give your niece a recorder for Christmas.

"You'll like this.
You gave it to me last year."

Toys would last so much longer if Dad was given his own.

"Right, now where are MY presents?"

The best presents
are those that can't be
bought.

Christmas dinner is
when you can avoid
talking by eating.

Christmas is great,
unless you're the turkey.

You don't get
fat between
Christmas and
New Year…

…just between
New Year and
Christmas.

"I much preferred it when we had turkey."

After a good meal you can
forgive anything…

...even your relatives.

Smile, it will all be over
in a few hours.

♟ ♟ ♟

"Anyone for the Queen's Speech?"

"This year I'm going to spend Christmas trolling people online."

No one gets out of here before Boxing Day.

Never ask your aunt
how she's getting on
with her music lessons.

"We always take Grandma out for a bit of exercise over Christmas."

It's great
when the
family visit,
and even
better when
they're gone.

ON THE FIRST DAY OF CHRISTMAS
MY TRUE LOVE AND ME...

...had Christmas lunch with my mum

…and then had Christmas dinner with my true love's dad and the new woman he met recently online.

ON THE SECOND DAY OF CHRISTMAS MY TRUE LOVE AND ME...

...drank more than we meant to at the neighbours' party.

ON THE THIRD DAY OF CHRISTMAS MY TRUE LOVE AND ME…

…drove two hours with a hangover to have Christmas dinner with the aunts.

On the fourth day of Christmas my true love and me...

...drove an hour and a half to have Christmas dinner with my true love's mum and her dull new husband and his brother and wife.

On the fifth day of Christmas my true love and me...

...visited my father, his wife, my brother and sister and had Christmas dinner and our usual political argument.

ON THE SIXTH DAY OF CHRISTMAS MY TRUE LOVE AND ME…

…had Christmas leftovers with the jolly cousins who live near my father and his family.

ON THE SEVENTH DAY OF CHRISTMAS MY TRUE LOVE AND ME...

...rather unwisely decided to see the New Year in with my brother and his family and friends.

ON THE EIGHTH DAY OF CHRISTMAS
MY TRUE LOVE AND ME ...

... met up with a friend from college we hadn't seen for years, and then remembered why we hadn't.

ON THE NINTH TO ELEVENTH DAY OF CHRISTMAS

MY TRUE LOVE AND ME…

…went to stay at my sister's
damp vegan collective
in mid-Wales…

…and went for a couple of
healthy damp walks.

On THE TWELFTH
DAY OF CHRISTMAS
MY TRUE LOVE
AND ME…

CHILLED OUT!

…before we had to get ready to
go back to work the next day…

Cath Tate has lived and worked in London for more years than she cares to mention. She currently runs a greetings card company, Cath Tate Cards, with her daughter Rosie: the bulk of the photos and captions in this book started life as greetings cards.

The photos have been collected over the years by Cath and her friends in junk shops and vintage fairs. They are all genuine and show people in all their glory, on the beach, on a day out, posing stiffly for the photographer, drinking with friends, smiling or scowling at the camera.

The photographs were mostly taken sometime between 1880 and 1960. Times change but people, their friendships, their little joys and stupid mistakes, remain the same. Some things have changed though, and Cath Tate has used modern technical wizardry to tease some colour into the cheeks of those whose cheeks lost their colour some time ago.

The quotes that go with the photos come from random corners of life and usually reflect some current concern that is bugging her.

If you want to see all the current greetings cards and other ephemera available from Cath Tate Cards see www.cathtatecards.com

Cath Tate

Many thanks to all those helped me put this book together, including Discordia, who have fed me with wonderful photos and ideas over the years, and Suzanne Perkins, who has made sure everything looks OK, and also has a good line in jokes.

Picture credits

Photos from the collection of Cath Tate apart from the following:

Discordia/Simon: Pages 18–19, 22–25, 38–41, 46–47, 54–57, 60–61, 64–65, 76–79, 84–87, 90–95, 98–105, 110–111

Discordia/Siegmann: Pages 44–45, 58–59, 62–63, 74–75, 106–107

Discordia/Kulturrecycling: Pages 30–31, 96–97

Keith Allen: Pages 10–11, 68–69